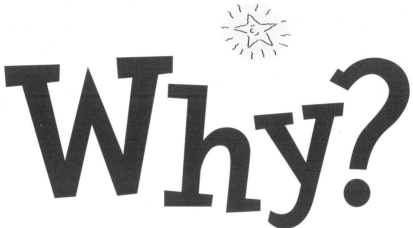

Why?

Why?

The best ever question and answer book about nature, science and the world around you

By Catherine Ripley
Illustrated by Scot Ritchie

Owl kids

For curious kids everywhere — and their parents — with the hope that this book helps to answer some of your wonderful "wonder why" questions. Keep asking! — C.R.

Owlkids Books acknowledges the financial support of the Canada Council for the Arts, the Ontario Arts Council, the Government of Canada through the Canada Book Fund (CBF) and the Government of Ontario through the Ontario Media Development Corporation's Book Initiative for our publishing activities.

Published in Canada by
Owlkids Books Inc.
10 Lower Spadina Avenue
Toronto, ON M5V 2Z2

Published in the United States by
Owlkids Books Inc.
1700 Fourth Street
Berkeley, CA 94710

Cataloguing data available from Library and Archives Canada

Library of Congress Control Number: 2010920479 (HC); 2017952469 (PB)

ISBN: 978-1-926818-00-9 (HC); 978-1-77147-321-7 (PB)

ONTARIO ARTS COUNCIL
CONSEIL DES ARTS DE L'ONTARIO
an Ontario government agency
un organisme du gouvernement de l'Ontario

Canada Council
for the Arts

Conseil des Arts
du Canada

Canadä

Manufactured in Shenzhen, Guangdong, China, in October 2017, by WKT Co. Ltd.
Job #17CB1550

F   G   H   I   J   K

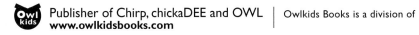 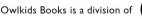 

Publisher of Chirp, chickaDEE and OWL
www.owlkidsbooks.com | Owlkids Books is a division of   Bayard
CANADA

Contents

Bathtime Questions

Supermarket Questions

Nighttime Questions

Outdoor Questions

Kitchen Questions

Farm Animal Questions

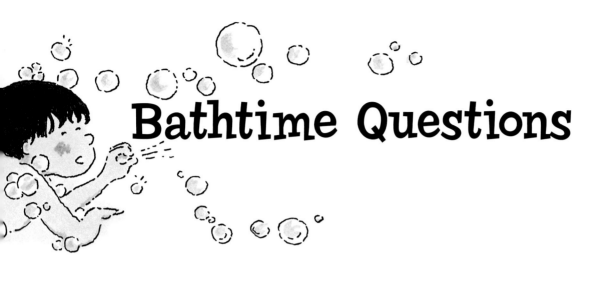

Bathtime Questions

11

How can hot and cold water run out of the same tap?

12

Surprise! Inside the wall behind the faucet there are two pipes. One pipe brings hot water from your hot water tank. The other pipe brings cold water directly from your neighborhood water supply. When you turn the tap, you let hot or cold water run into the faucet. Turn the tap a little and a trickle of water flows through, turn the tap a lot and water gushes out! If you let cold and hot water into the faucet at the same time, the water from the two pipes mixes together so that warm water runs out.

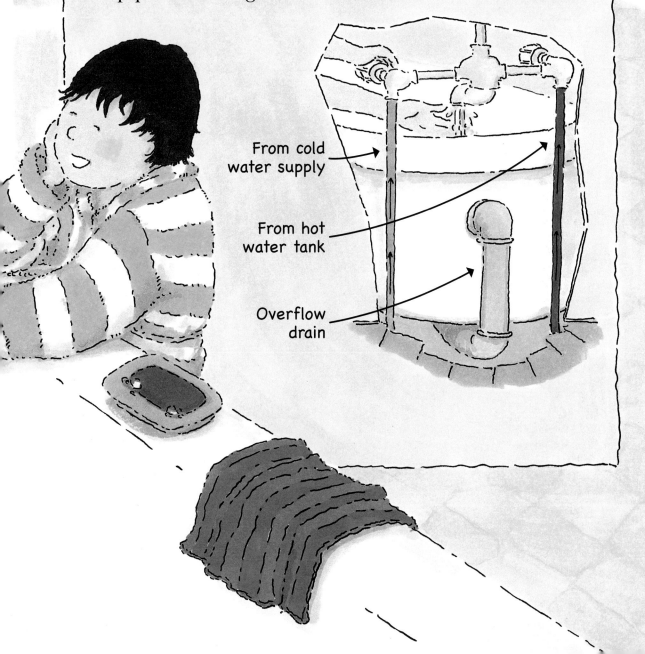

From cold
water supply

From hot
water tank

Overflow
drain

Why do I have to brush my teeth?

Inside your mouth are tiny, tiny living things called bacteria. When you don't brush, food sticks to your teeth and the bacteria eat the sugars in it. As they do, they let out waste that's full of acid strong enough to melt the hard outer coating of your teeth. Then, uh-oh, the acid makes holes! These holes are called cavities. By brushing your teeth, you get rid of the sugars that the bacteria like to eat. If the bacteria have nothing to eat, then there's no acid to make cavities in your teeth. That's why you brush.

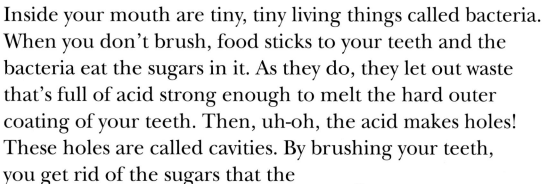

Why do I have to go to the bathroom?

To get rid of the leftovers. As you chew and swallow, your teeth and stomach turn, say, an apple into a soupy mush. The apple mush travels through your body becoming thinner and thinner. Some of it flows out of your small intestine into your blood and all around to feed the different body parts.

But there are always some leftovers! The leftover food mush in your large intestine becomes solid waste. Your kidneys take watery leftovers out of your blood, and send the liquid waste to your bladder. To get rid of all these leftovers, you go to the bathroom.

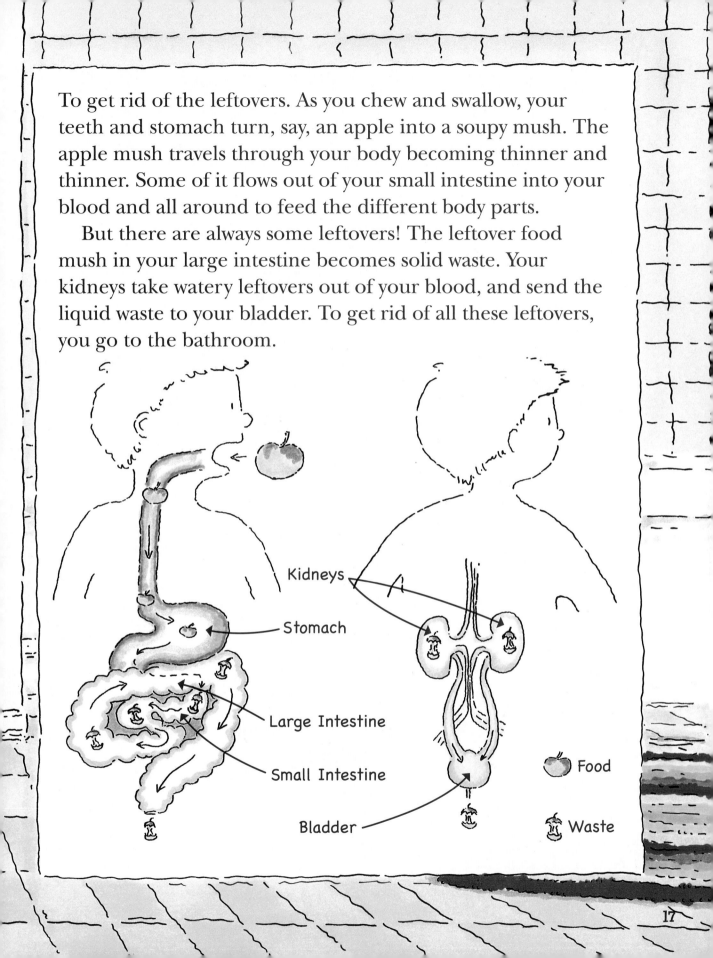

Kidneys

Stomach

Large Intestine

Small Intestine

Bladder

Food

Waste

Where does it go when I flush?

Down and out! Whoosh — the toilet water travels down a pipe from the toilet, through a pipe inside your home, and then out to a bigger pipe. If you live in the city, the water flows into an even bigger pipe under the street. Then it flows through bigger and bigger pipes on to a water treatment plant, where the toilet water is cleaned.

In the country, the pipe outside your house might carry the water into an underground septic tank, which is like a water treatment plant in your own backyard.

Water treatment plant

Pipes from houses

Animals don't have bathtubs — so how do they stay clean?

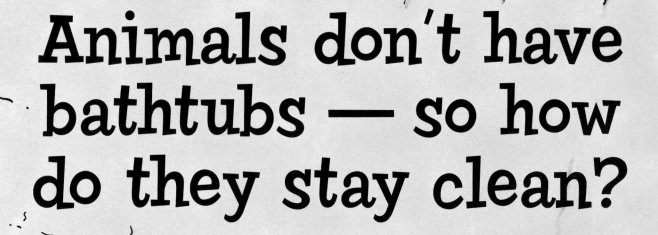

All sorts of ways. Believe it or not, zebras roll around in dirt to get clean! It's old skin and bugs they need to clean off. Chimps have a friend pick out the bugs and dirt from their hair, while cats use their tongues to lick themselves clean. Rhinos depend on the help of a special bird — the bird gets to have a meal of the pesky bugs it finds on the rhino's hide. And elephants shower or bathe in dust or in water — without the soap!

Why is soap so

All the better to clean you! Like all things, soap is made up of millions of molecules — tiny pieces so small you can't see them without a microscope. When soap gets wet, water molecules free up the soap molecules so that they can slip and slide around. They slip easily onto your skin, join with the dirt and slide the dirt right off your body, leaving you clean as a whistle.

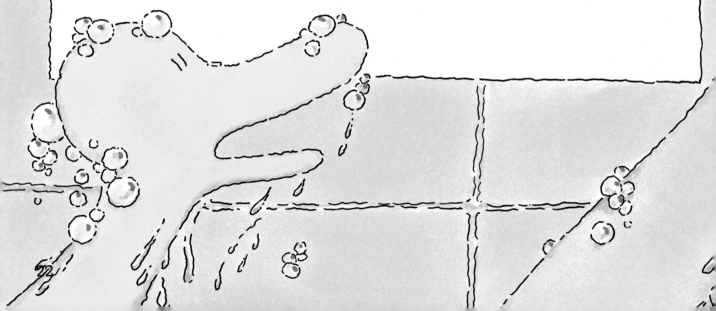

slippery?

Because they are not like the tears in your eyes. When shampoo gets in your eyes, your eyes feel the difference right away. They send a "stinging" message to your brain: *Ow! Help! Something strange is here!* To get rid of the strange stuff, the brain tells your eyes to make more tears and wash the shampoo away. Some shampoos are specially made to be as much like the water in your eyes as possible. These "tearless" shampoos fool your eyes and don't sting.

Because they get too naked! Your skin is covered by a thin, thin coat of oil. When you are in the bath for a long time, the coat of oil is washed away. The bath water can then seep under your naked skin, making it swell up and wrinkle. On the palms of your hands and the soles of your feet, the skin is thicker, so there's more skin to make big wrinkles.

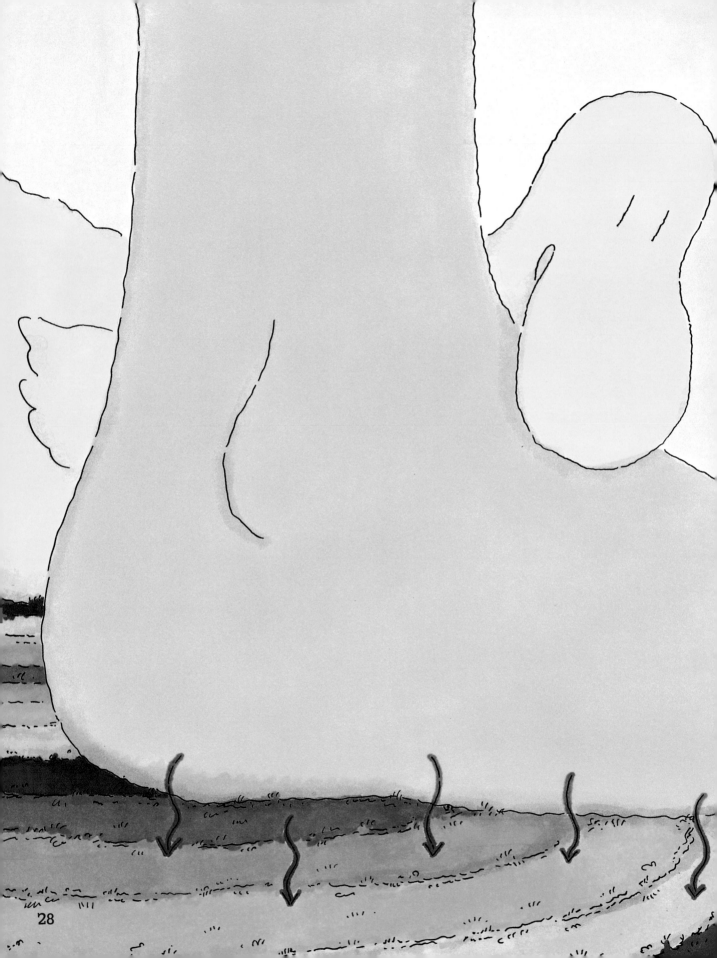

Why does the floor feel colder than the bathmat?

Because of the heat leaving your feet. The hard, smooth tile floor feels colder because it carries the heat away from your feet. The more the heat flows out of your feet, the colder they feel. The soft, fuzzy bathmat feels warmer because the spaces between the fuzz hold the heat, and don't pull it away from your feet as quickly as the tile floor does. And so, the bathmat feels warm and the floor feels cold.

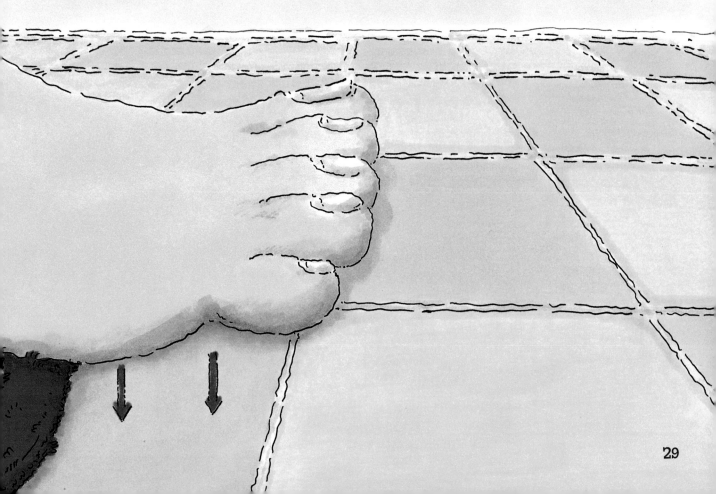

Why can I draw on the mirror?

Because the air is full of water. You usually can't see the water in the warm, wet air from your bath or shower. That's because the water is in its invisible form, called water vapor. But when water vapor lands on something colder than itself, like a mirror, it turns back into tiny drops of water. The drops make a thin layer, covering the mirror and making it white like a piece of paper. When you draw with your finger, it breaks the film apart to show the mirror underneath. Ta-da — a picture!

Why is there a funny noise when the water drains away?

Because the drainpipe is like an upside-down drinking straw. As you suck on a straw, you make an empty space, called a vacuum, inside it. When you get to the bottom of the glass, there isn't enough juice left to fill the space. Air rushes up the straw to help fill the space up. The juice and air slosh together and make a lot of noise. That's just what the last drops of water and air do when they rush down the drainpipe.

How do towels get dry by morning?

Because a drying towel is like a slo-o-o-o-o-w-ly boiling kettle. If you boil water in a kettle long enough, all the water will disappear. That's because the water turns into water vapor and leaves the kettle dry and empty. In the same way, if you leave a wet towel in a dry spot long enough, the water in the towel will slowly change into water vapor. Little by little, the invisible water vapor floats into the air and away from the towel, until it is dry.

Bath Bits

Ducks do more than just get clean when they preen, or run their feathers through their beaks. Their beaks carry oil from a gland at the back of their bodies and spread a thin coat of it all over, waterproofing their feathers.

Can you imagine disguising a bathtub as a tall set of dresser drawers? That's what some people did long ago to hide the bathtub in the bedroom. Why? Because there were no bathrooms yet!

When you blow a soap bubble, you fill a thin soap-and-water skin with enough air to make it float away.

Stop! Before you fill that glass to rinse your teeth, think about the fact that a dinosaur may have drunk that very same water millions of years ago. The water on Earth is used over and over and over and over....

Supermarket Questions

Do the doors open by magic?

No — without knowing it, you open them! Above the door, a special electronic "eye" sends down an invisible beam that spreads out in front of the door. When you walk through the beam, you break it. That tells a motor near the doors to start working, and to open the doors for you.

Where do apples come from in winter?

Some come from where it's summer, very far away. Others come from huge storerooms filled with — zzzzz — sleeping apples. Even after they are picked, apples use a gas in the air called oxygen, along with light and warmth, to get riper. Back in the fall, some apples were shut inside huge rooms. The rooms were kept cold and dark, and a special machine removed most of the oxygen from the air. So the apples fell asleep, and ripened very, very slowly. Months later, when workers took the apples out of the rooms to send to the store, they woke up fresh and crunchy.

45

Why does it smell so good here?

Because hot air rises. And there's a lot of hot air around when people are baking bread. Air rises inside the sticky bread dough as it bakes, making the bread light and fluffy. And some of the hot, steamy air rises out of the bread and floats through the air, right to your nose. The steam carries with it the smells of all the ingredients in the bread, mixed together to make that yummy bread smell. Once the baked goods are cooled and bagged, the air can't bring the smells to your nose as easily.

How does all this food get here?

In all kinds of trucks! Every day the supermarket manager orders food to sell at the store. Big transport trucks bring in the orders. Food that needs to be kept frozen or really cold comes in a truck that's like a giant freezer on wheels. Other refrigerated trucks are kept just cold enough to bring in milk and meat. Sometimes fresh-picked fruits and vegetables come from nearby farms in smaller pickup trucks. And snack foods like potato chips come in their very own — you guessed it! — transport truck!

What's behind the big doors?

Lots! Everything that keeps the workers working, the shelves stocked, the freezers full and the whole supermarket running is behind these doors. Turn the page to sneak a peek…

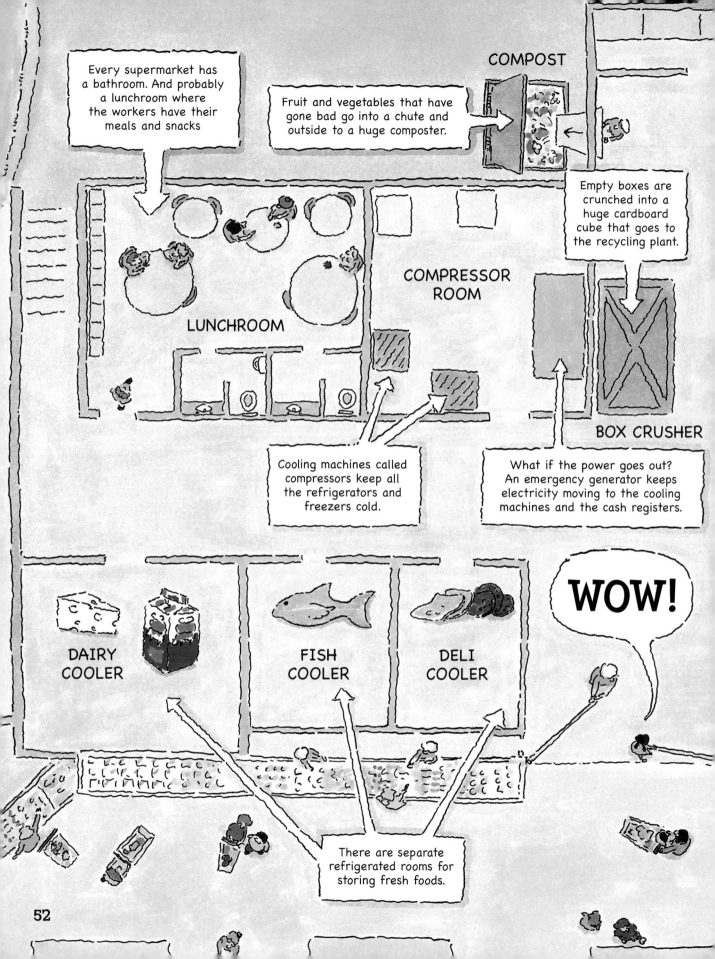

Every supermarket has a bathroom. And probably a lunchroom where the workers have their meals and snacks

COMPOST

Fruit and vegetables that have gone bad go into a chute and outside to a huge composter.

Empty boxes are crunched into a huge cardboard cube that goes to the recycling plant.

COMPRESSOR ROOM

LUNCHROOM

Cooling machines called compressors keep all the refrigerators and freezers cold.

BOX CRUSHER

What if the power goes out? An emergency generator keeps electricity moving to the cooling machines and the cash registers.

WOW!

DAIRY COOLER

FISH COOLER

DELI COOLER

There are separate refrigerated rooms for storing fresh foods.

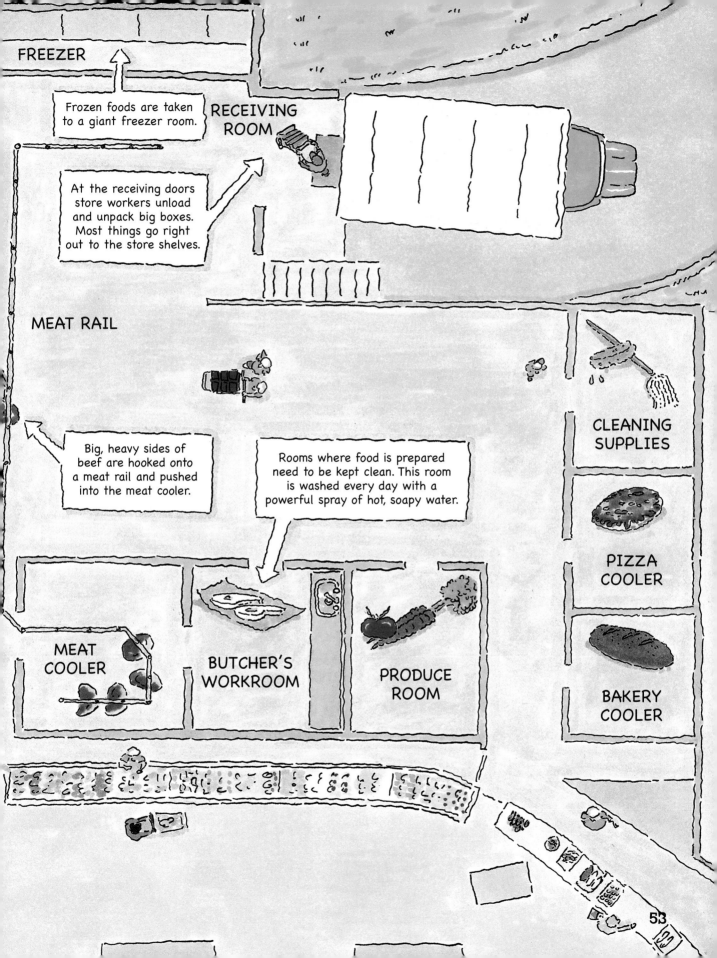

FREEZER

Frozen foods are taken to a giant freezer room.

RECEIVING ROOM

At the receiving doors store workers unload and unpack big boxes. Most things go right out to the store shelves.

MEAT RAIL

Big, heavy sides of beef are hooked onto a meat rail and pushed into the meat cooler.

Rooms where food is prepared need to be kept clean. This room is washed every day with a powerful spray of hot, soapy water.

CLEANING SUPPLIES

PIZZA COOLER

BAKERY COOLER

MEAT COOLER

BUTCHER'S WORKROOM

PRODUCE ROOM

What holds jelly dessert together?

Braids! But not the kind in your sister's hair — gelatin braids. Jelly powder contains gelatin that makes food thick and bouncy, plus sugar and other things to give it color and flavor. Bits of gelatin, so small you can't see them without a microscope, contain many tiny strands, like a braid. When boiling water dissolves the jelly powder, the gelatin braids come undone, and the strands get all mixed in with the water. Then, as the liquid cools, the gelatin pulls back together, trapping the water and sugar in between the strands. And that's what holds together this jiggly treat!

It depends on the type of chickens that laid them. White Leghorn chickens, for example, lay most of the white eggs that you can buy in a store. Brown eggs usually come from red hens. But there are all sorts of other chickens: some lay white eggs, some lay brown eggs, some lay speckled eggs, and the Ameraucana chicken from South America lays blue eggs!

How do they make spaghetti look like spaghetti and macaroni look like macaroni?

It's a story full of holes! In the noodle factory, the stiff pasta dough is pushed through holes in special metal plates. The shape of the pasta that comes out depends on the shape of the hole it was pushed through. When the dough is pushed through tiny holes, you get spaghetti. When it is pushed through round holes that have small pins in them, the dough comes out in long tubes. When the tubes are chopped into short pieces, you get macaroni.

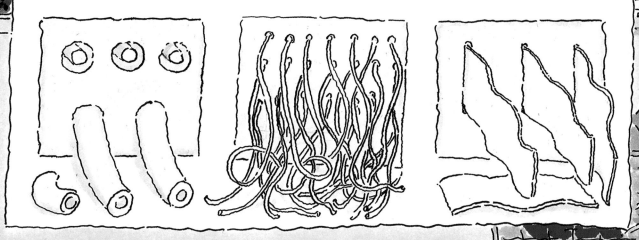

What puts the fizz in soda pop?

Thousands of tiny bubbles. Before soda pop is put in cans or bottles, it goes through a machine that makes it cold and presses on it. This makes it easy to fill the liquid with bubbles of a harmless gas called carbon dioxide. When you open a bottle or can of soda pop, the tiny bubbles begin to rush up to the top and burst. The fizz in your drink is lots of little bubbles bursting — pop, pop! Eventually all of the bubbles pop, and no more bubbles means no more fizz. Your soda pop has gone "flat."

Why do my fingers stick to the frozen juice cans?

Your fingers must be wet! When your fingers are even a little wet or sweaty and the cans are in a very, very cold freezer, you'll probably get stuck. As soon as you touch the can, the wetness on your skin freezes to the can, like an icy glue, and sticks your fingers to it. Brrrr!

Why do people bring their own bags to the store?

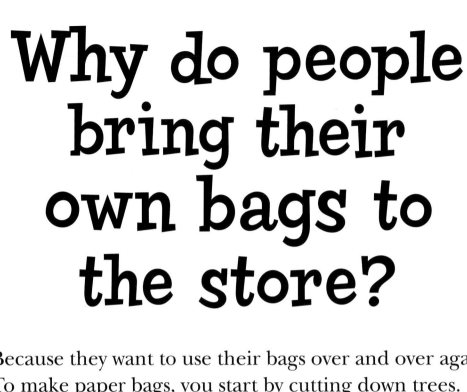

Because they want to use their bags over and over again. To make paper bags, you start by cutting down trees. To make plastic bags, you start by drilling for petroleum underground. Then lots of electricity is needed to make the trees and petroleum into bags. If you only use the bags once, they end up in the garbage and you have to start again. But if you reuse your bags again and again, or if you carry cloth or string bags that last a very long time, you won't waste trees, petroleum or electricity. And you won't add to the garbage.

Supermarket Bits

If the store doors don't open automatically for your little brother, it's probably because he's too short! The beam from the electronic eye gets weaker and wider the further it goes. A very short person doesn't break the beam, so the motor doesn't start and the doors don't open.

On most store items you'll find a Universal Product Code, or UPC. The bars and numbers are a code for the name and price of the product. If a store "scans" these bar codes into a computer, it gives you the information hidden in the codes. The information flashes on the cashier's screen, and then is printed on the cash register tape for you to take home.

Surprise — cheese comes from grass! Cows eat grass, and inside their bodies the grass gets turned into milk. After the cow is milked, some of the milk is used to make cheese. Ta-da — cheese from grass!

Nighttime Questions

71

Where does the sun go at night?

It doesn't go anywhere. It looks like it's gone, but it's still shining. We all live on the planet Earth, and it's the Earth — with you on it — that moves. Every day the Earth spins around once. The light from the sun only reaches the part of the Earth closest to it. Daytime happens when the part of the Earth you are on faces the sun. Nighttime happens when your part of the Earth spins away from the sun.

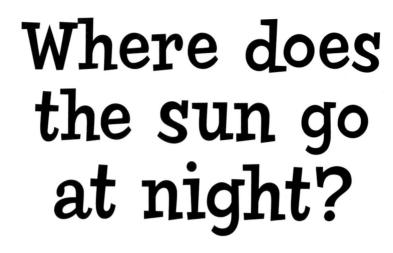

Moon

Sun

Earth

Why do a cat's eyes shine in the dark?

All the better to see with! Way inside a cat's eye are cells that act like a mirror. Light that shines on them is bounced back out. This gives the cat more light to see by in the dark night. When you see a cat's eyes shining in the dark, you are seeing light being reflected back out.

Is there a man in the moon?

Not really. The lines and curves that look like eyes and a nose and a mouth are really mountains and plains on the moon's surface. Moon mountains are made up of light-colored rock. Moon plains are made of dark rock. The bright mountains and dark plains make up the pattern of a man's face in the moon.

Or is it a rabbit?   Or is it a crab?   Or is it a lady?

Why do tulips close up at night?

Because the insides of the flower are very important. That's where new seeds come from. Tulips bloom in spring when nights — brrr! — can be cool and frosty. Cold can hurt the parts inside the flowers, so the flowers close up tight to protect their insides from the cold. When it is warmer during the day, the tulips open up again. Then bees can get inside the flowers to help start new seeds growing. And from new seeds come new flowers.

To wake up your brain! To stay active and alert, your brain needs lots of a gas called oxygen. Oxygen is in the air you breathe, and gets sent all around your body in your blood. After a busy day, your heart pumps blood more slowly than before. Your sleepy brain needs more oxygen. YA-A-A-WNNN! You gulp in a lot of air and the oxygen it contains, and your brain feels better.

Why do stars twinkle?

Because of blankets of air. Earth is surrounded by its atmosphere — piles of thin layers or blankets of air. Starlight has to come through the atmosphere for us to see it. It travels in beams from so far away that the beams are weak by the time they get here. They run into humps and bumps in the atmosphere. The light beams move back and forth a little — and the stars seem to wink and twinkle!

Why doesn't that bird fall off the branch?

It is locked into place. Long tendons, or cords, run all the way down the inside of a bird's legs to its toes. To settle on a branch, the bird bends its legs. Bending pulls the tendons. The tendons pull on the toes, making them curl around the branch. As long as the bird is perched on the branch, its legs are bent. As long as its legs are bent, its toes are locked in place.

Tendon

Toes

What's under my bed?

Some toys, a shoe, a book, a sock... and dust mites. Dust mites are tiny creatures so small you can't see them. But if you could shrink down thousands and thousands of times, you'd see dust mites under there, munching away. They chew on tiny flakes of dead skin and loose hair in the dust, and they sure do a good job of cleaning up!

Why do I have to sleep?

No one really knows for sure. Some scientists think you need a time when all the parts of your body can slow down and rest. Others think that sleep also gives your body a chance to make repairs, like healing a cut, and to get back the energy you use during a busy day. Whatever the reason, sleeping must be something you have to do, or you wouldn't get sleepy!

Why can't I see just after the light goes out?

Because your eyes aren't ready for the dark yet. The dark-colored opening in the middle of your eye — the pupil — lets in light so you can see. In the dark, your pupils have to open up wider to catch what little light there is. When the lights first go out, it takes a few seconds for your pupils to widen. Until they do, you can't see much and everything looks completely black.

What makes that toy glow in the dark?

Dancing particles! All things are made up of particles, such as electrons, neutrons and protons, that are so small you can't see them without a powerful microscope. Glow in the dark toys include electrons that get excited by light. Light makes them move and bump and dance. When they bump together, they start to shine. This makes the toy glow. You can see it glow in the dark when the lights go out.

Will I dream tonight?

Absolutely. You dream many, many dreams every single night — even if you don't remember them when you wake up. Scientists think that you dream as your brain tries to make sense of all the things you've done and felt during the day. They also think that animals dream, just like you do. Sweet dreams!

Nighttime Bits

Lots of creatures are busy at night when other animals sleep. After dark, bats come out to catch bugs while daytime birds are snoozing. When daylight comes, bats hang upside-down to sleep while birds fly around catching bugs.

Tick, tick, tick. Even if you can't see a real clock, your body knows it's bedtime at the end of the day. You have a sort of inner clock that senses how much light is around. Less light means it's time to sleep, so your body makes melatonin, a substance that makes you sleepy.

A shooting star isn't a star at all. It's really a meteor, a rock from outer space that burns as it zooms down through the Earth's atmosphere. Flash! Most meteors are pea-sized or smaller, and burn up before they hit the ground.

Outdoor Questions

Why does it smell so fresh after it rains?

Because the air is clean and wet. First the rain washes floating bits, like dust and soot, out of the air. Then the wetness keeps the bits down on the ground, so they don't get in the way of you sniffing other stuff. Wet air carries the smells of the wet trees, grass and earth to your nose better than dry air does. The moisture in the air even makes the inside of your nose wetter, the better to trap all those fresh smells!

Why do worms come out when it's wet?

Because worms like it wet! If worms don't stay a little wet, their skin dries out and they can't breathe. When it is sunny or very dry, they stay underground in the moist soil. But when it rains, worms don't have to worry about drying out. Out they squirm. They may be looking for more air to breathe or a mate or a new place to live. Or, maybe, the shake of the soil from the raindrops falling attracted them up and out. Whatever the reason, a soggy day is a good day for worms to be wriggling around above ground!

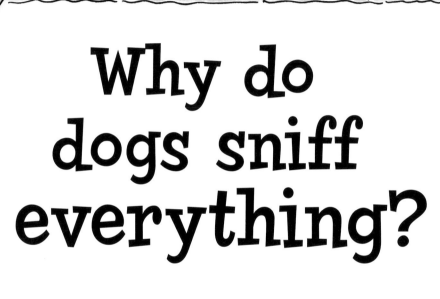

Why do dogs sniff everything?

Sniff-sniff-sniffing is a dog's way of checking things out. A dog's nose can smell things about forty times better than your nose can. By sniffing, a dog can tell who has been around its home area recently. It can tell if there is another dog nearby. It can tell if the animals it meets (and that includes you) are afraid or happy. A dog also sniffs to find food or to hunt down an interesting-smelling animal, such as a rabbit or — meow — a cat!

Ow! How does my cut stop bleeding?

It's a sticky story. As soon as you cut yourself, parts of your blood called platelets start to gather. They stick to each other and to the edges of your cut, forming a thin cover over it. If the cut is big, the platelets may need extra help to stop the bleeding. Along comes fibrin to the rescue. Fibrin is another special part of your blood. It weaves a criss-crossing tangle of long, sticky strands over the cut. Then the strands dry out to make a scab. The scab acts like a bandage, and lets new skin grow underneath. So whatever you do, don't pick at it!

Why do dandelions turn white and fluffy?

So they can make more dandelions! Every dandelion bloom is made up of more than a hundred tiny yellow flowers. A seed forms inside each flower, and gets attached to a long stalk. At the top of the stalks are white tufts. When the yellow petals fall off, all you see is a white ball of fluff. The fluffy tufts are like little kites, each carrying a seed. Along comes the wind, and carries the tufts and their seeds far and wide. The seeds get spread all around, and every seed could grow into a new dandelion.

Why is the sky blue?

Because of scattered blue light waves. Believe it or not, clear light is made up of all the colors in the rainbow — red, orange, yellow, green, blue, indigo and violet. These colors travel in waves. When light hits things, some of the color waves are soaked up, and others bounce off. Whatever waves bounce back to your eyes, those are the colors you see!

High in the sky, the waves of light from the sun hit the air. Air is made up of different gases in tiny, tiny bits called molecules. The blue light waves bounce off these bits of air, and scatter all over the sky. So when you look up, it's blue as far as you can see.

What's that white line in the sky?

It's a trail of ice! It shows you where a jet plane has been. Jet planes have engines to make them move. As the engines work, they let off exhaust that includes water so hot it's like steam coming out of a kettle. When the hot exhaust hits the air outside the plane, the steam cools and turns into water droplets. A second later, the water droplets turn into ice in the fre-e-e-e-zing cold air way up high. These little pieces of ice make a long, white trail behind the plane as it moves.

Why do I feel funny inside when I swing?

Because you're out of balance. It all starts deep in your ears. Messages go from here to your brain. They tell your brain which way you're going and how fast you're going. That's how you keep your balance. When you swing, your body changes its place so fast, the messages can't keep up. Your brain gets a little confused. And when your brain is a little confused, you might feel mixed up inside. The same thing can happen on a roller coaster or even an elevator — whee!

Why do some rocks sparkle?

Because parts of the rock are as smooth as a mirror. Even if a rock looks rough, some of its very small parts can be smooth and flat. When light hits something smooth, some of it bounces off. Just think of how light shines off a mirror. And the more smooth parts the light has to bounce off, the more sparkles it makes. So rocks with lots of little smooth parts really sparkle and shine.

Why do birds sing?

They're talking! If birds sang in words, you'd hear a lot of different messages. In springtime you might hear a male bird's song that says both "Stay away" and "Come and be my sweetie." To other male birds, it's a message to keep out of the singing bird's area, but female birds hear the same call as an invitation to come right in! Birds sing out all kinds of messages. Baby birds call "I'm hun-hun-hungry, Mom and Dad!" Birds in a flock will call to stay together, singing "I'm here, but where are you?" Some birds will even warn each other of danger, calling "Watch out, watch out wherever you are!" All in bird talk, of course.

What's a shadow?

It's where light isn't. Light can't travel through things that get in its way. For example, when sunlight hits you, it's stopped by your body, while all around you it reaches the ground. Where you block light from reaching the ground, a dark shape is formed...your shadow! It goes with you everywhere — see for yourself on a sunny day.

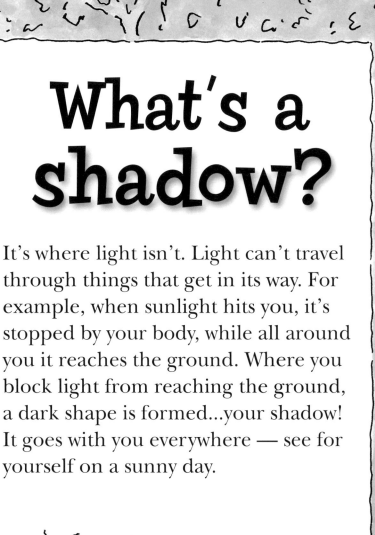

Where do puddles go?

Up, down and all around. Sometimes a thirsty animal will lap up some of the puddle water, so the puddle gets smaller. Much of the water seeps down out of sight into the soil. When it stops raining, what's left of a puddle starts to dry up. The water floats away into the air all around, like water from wet clothes hanging up to dry. Going, going, gone!

Outdoor Bits

Some clouds look like giant cotton balls, just right for jumping into. Not really! Jumping into a cloud would be like jumping into fog — cold, damp and clammy. Clouds are made of millions and millions of tiny drops of cold water, and sometimes tiny ice crystals, too.

It's raining...hamburgers? Raindrops are nice and round way up high in the clouds. But as they fall to Earth, the air pushing against them flattens them into mini hamburger-shaped drops!

Have you ever noticed that dogs pee a little in a lot of places? Like their relatives the wolves, dogs do this to mark out an area as their home. When other dogs sniff these spots, they know they have to behave in this dog's home area, get out or fight to stay and be top dog.

Kitchen Questions

Why does my tummy g-r-r-rowl?

It's air rumbling around inside you. Inside your body, your stomach and intestines are always moving. When you eat, the movement mashes your food into soupy goop that your body can use to feed itself. But what happens when there is no more food left to mash up? Your stomach and intestines push around the air inside. Rumble, grumble.

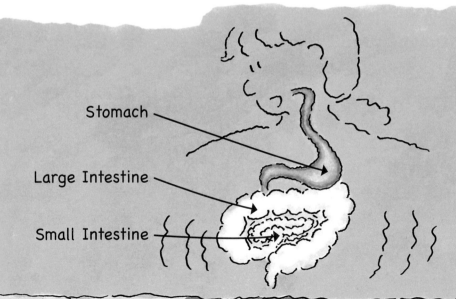

Stomach

Large Intestine

Small Intestine

Why does popcorn pop?

Popcorn kernels are hard on the outside. But on the inside they are soft and a little bit wet. When you heat up the kernels, the water inside heats up, too. It turns into a puff of hot steam that's trapped inside the kernel. The steam pushes from inside until the kernel explodes! The hard outer coat bursts open and the kernel turns inside out. Pop!

Children under the age of 5 should eat foods like popcorn only with supervision, to prevent the chances of choking.

Why are peaches fuzzy?

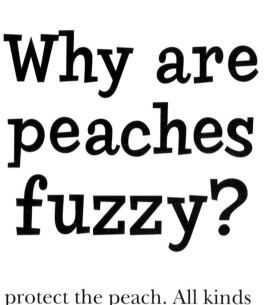

To protect the peach. All kinds of fruit — smooth apples, bumpy oranges, prickly pineapples and fuzzy peaches — have skin to help them stay healthy. Each type of skin keeps out insects or sickness or whatever it is that might hurt that kind of fruit. For example, peach fuzz stops a sickness called brown rot from touching the peach skin and rotting the fruit. The fuzzier the peach, the better!

Why does dish soap bubble so much?

Because there's more soap than dirt. When soap and water mix together, they make a film. It traps bits of dirt and slides them off the dirty dishes. But if there's more soap than dirt, the extra soap film traps bits of air. Soap film with air inside makes bubbles! The people who make dish soap know that we like lots of bubbles, so they put in a lot of extra soap. Lots of soap means you get tons of bubbles.

How does the fridge keep food cold?

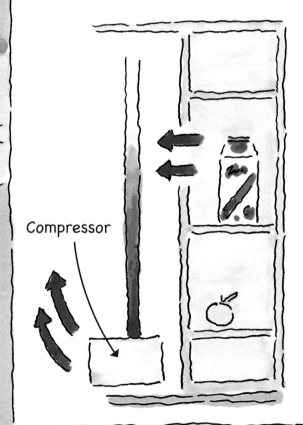

Compressor

By taking out the heat. The refrigerator has a long pipe in its walls. A motor, called a compressor, pumps special stuff through the pipe. The stuff collects the heat from inside the fridge where the food is. Then the fridge lets out the heat into the kitchen. By taking away the heat, the fridge keeps everything inside cool and frosty.

Why do onions make you cry?

Because you've cut them open. Onions, like all plants and animals, are made up of tiny cells you need a microscope to see. When you peel or cut an onion, you cut through these cells and they release a gas. You can't see it, but your eyes can feel it! The gas stings your eyes, so they make tears to wash the gas away.

What makes food sizzle?

Dancing water drops! There is water inside food. When you put it in a hot pan, the water comes out in tiny drops. As soon as they hit the hot pan, the drops dance around, exploding into little puffs of steam. Dancing and exploding, they make little waves in the air that travel to your ears as a sizzling sound.

Why does garbage smell?

There must be food rotting in there. That means that tiny, tiny creatures called bacteria are breaking down the food. As they work on the food, some of them let out a smell. Pee-yoo! Good thing, because eating rotten food can make you sick.

Where does glass come from?

From the beach! That's because glass is made from sand. Sand is put in a really hot furnace with some other stuff, and it melts. Glassmakers take the red-hot liquid and shape it — carefully. When the glass cools down, it can harden into drinking glasses, or windows, or sunglasses or...

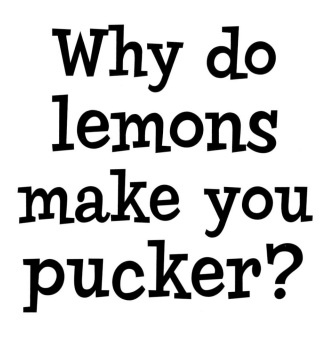

Why do lemons make you pucker?

Because they are so sour. When you put lemon in your mouth, saliva takes the sharp juice to the taste buds inside your tongue. Taste buds send a message to your brain saying, "Too sour!" Your brain sends back a message to wash away the juice with more saliva. The saliva goes all over as your mouth squeezes and twists and puckers!

Why do ice cubes crack?

They're trying to shrink! When water freezes, it gets bigger and lighter. As soon as you put an ice cube in a drink, the outside of the cube wants to turn back into water. So the cube tries to shrink — quickly! The shrinking squeezes hard on the inside of the ice cube and, all of a sudden, the inside part goes crack!

How does blowing on food cool it off?

When you see steam rising from hot food, it's because heat is coming out. The steam acts like a blanket that helps keep the heat in. The faster you blow the blanket of steam away, the faster the heat can leave the food, and the faster the food cools down. Puff, puff, puff — yum!

Kitchen Bits

A special strip of metal inside your toaster makes your toast pop up. The heat makes part of the strip get bigger and bigger. The strip triggers a spring. The spring lets go of the bar the toast is sitting on. And up POPS your toast!

A long time ago, there was no electricity to run fridges. How did people keep their food cold on a hot summer day? They put it in an "ice box" with a big block of ice. The ice was cut from lakes or rivers in the water and stored in sawdust to keep it frozen.

Is it sugar or salt? It's hard to tell without tasting. Sugar is sweet because it comes from plants, like sugarcane and sugar beets. Salt is a mineral that is dried out of sea water or is dug out of mines underground.

Farm Animal Questions

160

Why do ducks waddle?

They'd rather be swimming than walking around!
A duck's body is wide. Its legs are far apart and
back near its tail. Its feet are webbed. Perfect for
swimming — which ducks do a lot of the time — but
not so good for walking. Waddle, waddle, splash!

How does a chick get out of the egg?

It pecks its way out. After 21 days inside an egg, a chick gets big. It needs more space, and is ready to breathe fresh air. Using its egg tooth, a special bump on the end of its beak, it pecks a tiny hole. Peck, peck, peck. Finally the egg starts to crack. Chip, pip, peck! A few hours later, out comes a tired, wet chick. Soon the chick is dry and fluffy, and a day later its egg tooth falls off.

Why does a bunny's fur feel so soft?

Each hair is thin and bends easily. That's why it's soft. Rabbits have two types of hair: short underfur and guard hairs on top. The shorter the guard hairs, the softer they feel. Fur that isn't dry and rough also means healthy fur, so you must be petting a healthy, short-haired rabbit.

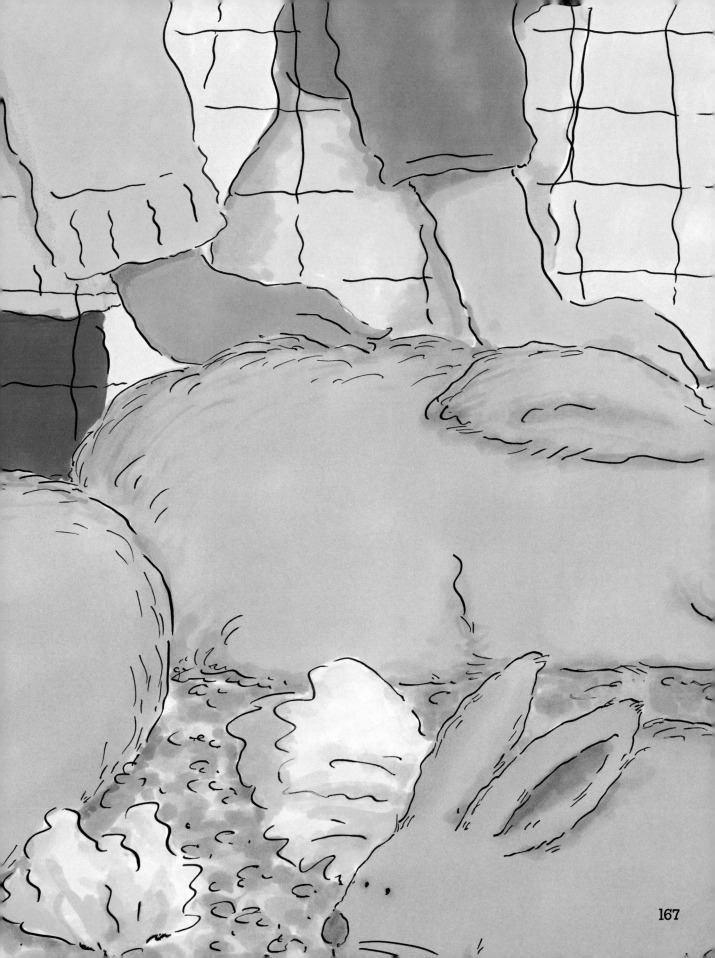

What's a ewe?

A mother sheep. A father sheep is called a ram, and a baby sheep is called a lamb. We give male, female and young animals different names. How many of these animal names do you know?

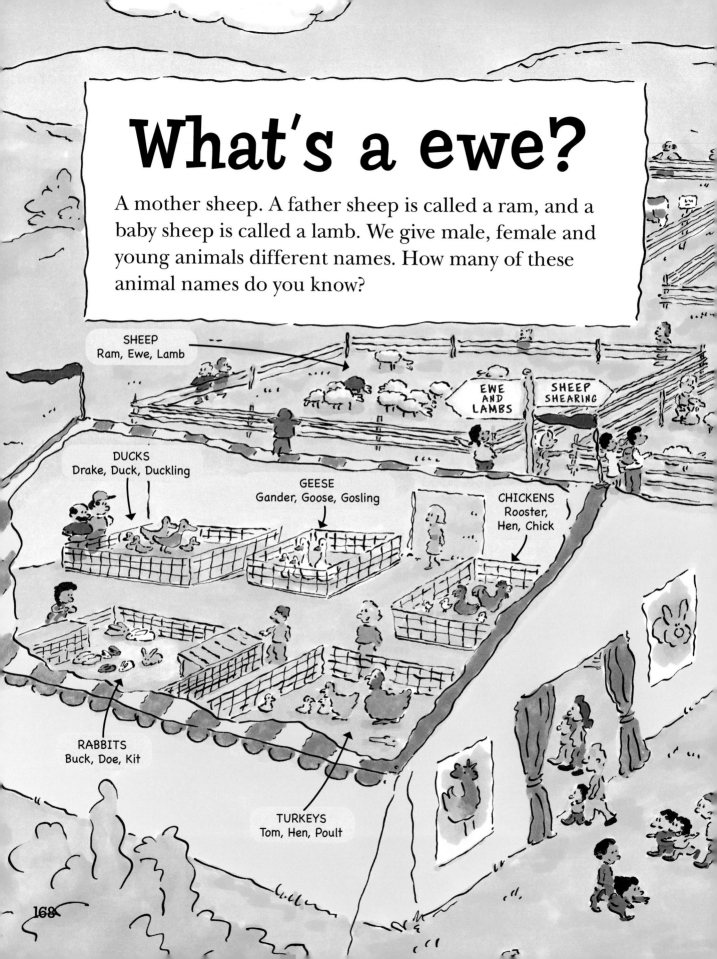

SHEEP
Ram, Ewe, Lamb

EWE AND LAMBS

SHEEP SHEARING

DUCKS
Drake, Duck, Duckling

GEESE
Gander, Goose, Gosling

CHICKENS
Rooster, Hen, Chick

RABBITS
Buck, Doe, Kit

TURKEYS
Tom, Hen, Poult

COWS
Bull, Cow, Calf

HORSES
Stallion, Mare, Foal

BEES
Queen bee,
Drone (male),
Worker (female),
Larva (young)

GOATS
Billy, Nanny, Kid

PIGS
Boar, Sow, Piglet

Why are sheep shaved?

To keep them cool and clean, and to get the wool to sell. It's hard to shear the wool off in one big piece! The wool is washed, untangled and spun into long strands of yarn — sometimes by hand, but usually in big machines. The yarn can be knitted or woven into clothes or blankets. During the year the sheep grow back their woolen coats and then — baaaa! — it's sheep shearing time again in the spring.

Why do cows moo?

They're talking! One way animals talk to each other is by making sounds — baaa-ing, quacking, woofing, oinking and moooooo-ing. Dairy cows moo or "bawl" if milking time is late, to tell the farmer their udders are getting too full of milk. They also moo if they're hungry. Out in the pasture, beef cows with calves moo to keep their babies close and safe.

What are the cows chewing?

Their cuds. A cow eats hay, grain or grass. Its huge stomach has four parts. The food is formed into balls or cuds in the second part, the reticulum. Muscles there move and send the cuds, one by one, back to the cow's mouth. Chew, chew! The cow breaks down the cuds, then swallows again. Now the well-chewed food moves on through the rest of the cow's stomach.

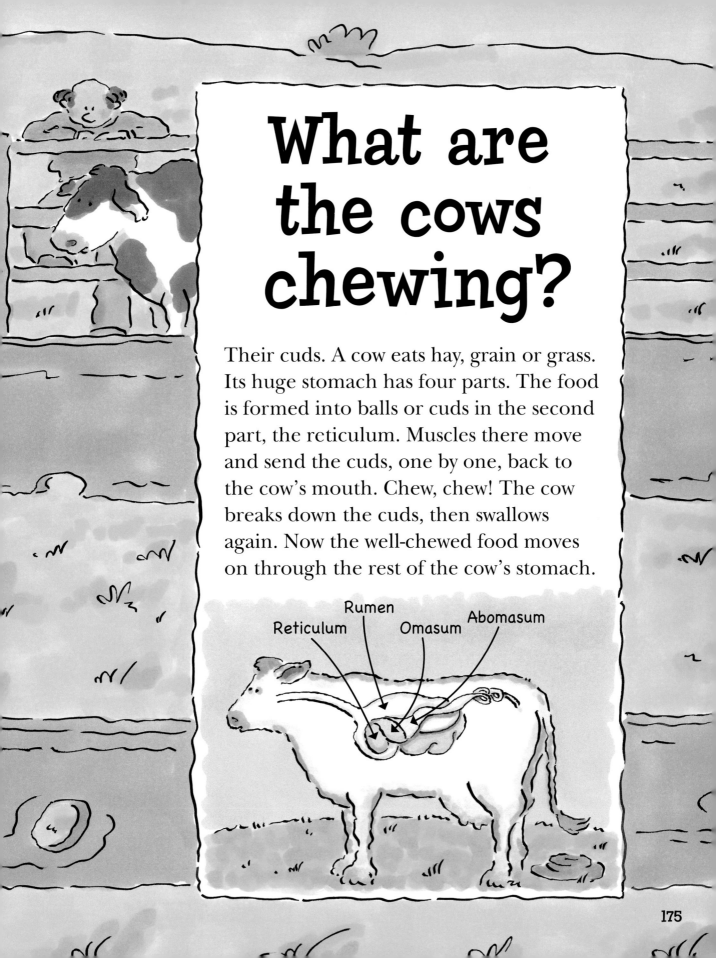

Reticulum   Rumen   Omasum   Abomasum

Why do horses swish their tails?

To flick away the flies. Horn flies, stable flies, horse flies, house flies, black flies, mosquitoes and other insects all bother and bite horses. Bzzz! Bite! Sometimes the insects can pass on germs that make horses sick. So the horse uses its tail to keep the flies from landing on its skin.

Why do horses sleep standing up?

For a fast getaway. Today, most horses live in stables. But long ago they all lived in the wild. They were hunted by wolves, mountain lions, coyotes and bears. To stay safe and alive, horses had to be able to run away from danger FAST! Just two hours after a foal is born, it is ready to run. Horses can take off faster from a standing position than from a lying-down position, and that's why horses sleep standing up.

Why do only some goats have horns?

Because they haven't been de-horned. Many goats are born ready to grow horns. Horns are hard and have no feeling — sort of like your fingernails. In the wild, goats use them to protect themselves, to show off and to fight. But on a farm, sharp horns can be dangerous to people and other animals. When kids are a few days old, many farmers stop the horns from starting to grow.

How do bees make honey?

They dry out nectar. Nectar is sweet, watery liquid that bees collect from flowers. The bees take the nectar to the hive to be put in tiny openings in the honeycomb called cells. Bees fan the nectar with their wings. They stir it and move it from cell to cell, mixing it with older nectar. As the nectar slowly dries, it thickens. Then, when the cell is full, the bee seals it off with a wax cap. Mmmmm, honey!

Why do pigs roll in the mud?

To stay cool and comfortable. When it's hot out, you sweat to stay cool. But pigs can't sweat. You put on sunscreen to protect your skin from burning and use bug stuff for the bugs, but pigs can't do that. The barn keeps animals cool, clean and bug-free, but what do pigs do outside? Roll in the mud! It protects their skin from sunburn and bug bites, and it keeps them cool, too.

Farm Bits

Is that chicken eating dirt? A chicken doesn't have teeth to grind up its food. So it swallows stones and bits of dirt. In a part of the chicken called the gizzard, the stones grind and mash down the food the chicken has swallowed.

Rabbits are always wiggling their noses. In the wild, rabbits need to be on the lookout for danger. They use their long ears to hear every sound, and move their noses to catch smells from every direction. Wiggle, twitch.

Grain and hay is kept to feed the farm animals or to sell. Rats and mice eat the grain and hay, and sometimes pass on sicknesses, too. So farmers usually have a lot of — meow! — barn cats around to catch rats and mice.

Index